CELLAR TESTAMENT

ACKNOWLEDGMENTS

I'm grateful to the following publications, in which some of these poems originally appeared:

Beloit Poetry Journal, for "Sorry as We Are."

Map Literary, for "Burning Man."

Zone 3, for "Not Much More Than a Mouth."

And I'm so grateful to my family and friends who saw me through while I was writing *Cellar Testament.* This book is for them.

ABOUT THE AUTHOR

Greg Glazner's books of poetry are *From the Iron Chair* and *Singularity,* both published by W.W. Norton. His awards include The Walt Whitman Award, The Bess Hokin Award from *Poetry,* and an NEA Fellowship. He teaches at UC Davis and in the low-residency MFA program at Pacific Lutheran University.

CELLAR TESTAMENT

by Greg Glazner

Winner of the 2018 Rachel Wetzsteon Chapbook Award

Copyright © 2018 Greg Glazner
All rights reserved.
ISBN: 1727314336
ISBN-13: 978-1727314335

The Rachel Wetzsteon Chapbook Award honors the memory of our esteemed poet, editor, professor, and colleague at William Paterson University. The award rotates annually to include poetry, fiction, and nonfiction.

Map Literary is dedicated to celebrating quality works of new literature. Rather than aligning with any one aesthetic, we aspire to promote the finest provocative writing of our time.

EDITOR
John Parras

Layout and typeset by Eric J. Scholz

Cover photograph by Chris Kridler

The William Paterson University of New Jersey
College of Humanities and Social Sciences
Department of English
300 Pompton Road
Wayne, NJ 07470

www.mapliterary.org

Is that the storm's heart? The ground is unstilling itself.
—Roethke, "The Lost Son"

CONTENTS

I	Ghost You In	3
II	Hover Near	7
III	Not Much More Than a Mouth	13
IV	Sorry as We Are	19
V	Burning Man	25

Ghost You In

    1.
Anymore the drowning and yelling out asleep
are through
                and I can last down here all
morning by these candles.
                          True the citronella
burns the lungs   and I blow the flames
out from time to time
                     breathing
by bulb light and the whine
of mosquitoes in the seep
                          or I open the iron
door overhead a good while
to the sun.
            But when I wrestle it
back down shut by god

no storm or call of any
magnitude could ever have me.

    2.
I put another struck match
to the wicks
                the zag-shaped oak stick
I've laid across a metal cup of water
wavering in gold
                      and call you back
by flickerings and shadow
by the jobs and names you went by
                            diviner
yes or dowser when by story
water witcher if paid
Jim Roy to your kin.
                      Once you laid your hands
over my young grip on a forked
branch you'd cut
                and a pasture's whole
underworld of water reached up to us
to bend it down.
            Arrive by voice
Jim Roy I'm listening

    by tug or glow I'm wide wake
                          and if the violence
comes with you the iron door's
bolted from inside.
                What is this calling
that destroys you? What's a person
stripped all the way down?

I ghost you name by title
branch by cupful by flame.
                    You vanished knowing
and I need to ghost you in.

3.
Leaves thrashed the windows   a gray-green
downpour   you glanced over
                        a mass on the radar
blotting out the town name   Lawton   the TV
sound off   steel guitar going on the radio.
You looked back
                the wet blast   the branches
stripped bare. All the effects you'd lived by
dimmed indifferently
                    countertops of pipe glue
and fittings   Fleet and Mule kenneled in the hall
the small table with Ava's letter open there.
You could feel a call
                funneling upward
strong as all the water that had ever pulled
from underground.
                You moved toward
the noise   some force of wind or hand
had the front door open
                  and you were through.

4.
Your mouth blown wide the work jacket
beating you the tired weight
on your feet coming off
your mind swelling into the brain-shaped

thunderheads your thirst drawn up
to the cure more water up there
than air you'd say *Wasn't no pull*
in a branch ever truer
                         all of a piece
now all one calling and called to
driving the sparse oaks and cedars down together
widening and pouring and lighting up
whole counties for your moment

until you go black and fall—

5.
I grope up for the string and pull the bulb on
choking back the coughing. Blown smoke

hazes the look of the radio
and batteries   the cans of soup
the plastic water jugs.
                       Now the first
high whine arrives to mock the asking.
As if that mattered   practiced as I am
at the laughable.
                       So Jim Roy when your flash
is over and you're thrashed down
to your pulse
              what is it you've become
what kind of mumbling drifter
through what world?
                   Maybe you won't say
but spill the cup   or kill the power
in time I'll see. Right now
the choking has me.
                  I climb to the door
clearing my throat   and open it
letting smoke evaporate
keeping an eye
             on the high white
underbellies gathering in the blue
until there's air enough
               to go back down.

HOVER NEAR

1.
Shadow blind   half-tranced   trying not to
cough on the wicks
                I'm breathing you in
with the air   shade or djin   whatever you are
brooding yourself to life
                filling the cellar
with weather.
          Here are my eyes and voice
my wince and stammer   everything I've heard
or guessed.
          Help yourself to what you need
and we'll move through this if we can
kinsman   twin
           pulled to whatever
makes it easier to live again.

2.
The staggered   feeling their way   the bruised of brain
the desperate for their bearings all pull   if raggedly
toward the portal to the storied
                    under the ancient
fluorescents rearward in the feed store. You hover
there at the shadowy edge   keeping the weight
off your injuries
           waiting to be called in as if by dream—
the four usuals faintly greened around the flecked
Formica table   the owner   Shell   spinning her domino
face-down
       saying *That old boy that diviner*
the men already coughing and laughing
into their hands   their various sags and heat-marks
shaking
      I guess he taken a blown-off
door and crawled under it out back of here
half her face slack   the other
                         half smiling.

Stroke or bludgeoning hail   pipe crush or calling—
if surviving whatever drops you
is most of the joke
                    I get it. But I'd go a long
long way with you to get the rest.

3.
The pasteboard door slides
half off and you sit up
squinting.
            What world is this?
All the black has been daylit
out of the clouds
                and the lightsources
of the alleyway mesquites are on
their shattered dark branches   their bright
clumps of green.
                Three radiant aluminum
trashcans are mashed on their sides
in the hail
        a drift of it against you
the rivered street beyond. You reach
to the horizon
            the thin morning clouds.
Something worldwide still has you
some pull   a calling
                so wincing
you shove the rest of the door off you
stand up soaked and mudded

and limp on uphill half-smiling.

4.
If I wheeze or choke too long   if I kill
the flames and pull the bulb light
on in here
            maybe you'll lapse to less
than a ghost again in air
                    maybe you're already
passing on what's coming.

                        Remembering all that hope
you'd say   opening your beard so your mouth
and teeth showed   *is a whole lot sorrier*
than to just forget about it
                              and kinsman
I'm listening. But shuffling
ahead arm-in-arm
                    leaning on a good leg each
isn't it possible we'd stand up
straight again together?

5.
Stems and worms scrawl themselves
across the curb you walk
                          stepping high
with one foot to spare them
the flapping leather. You catch
the eye of a hopping crow   the quick
sidelong nod.
              What is this?
Patterns you can still half-read
in the original   bird weeds
and street current   swirl on each side
of your curb.
              You can't tell
what you are anymore   and what was gale
can't believe what the street is
that it speaks
              so ceaselessly as you cross it
lumber floating at your ankles   bright plastics
three species of drowned birds you follow
bruised behind the eyes and knowing

things it isn't feasible to say. So you
make your way by wet sidewalk
                                humming
now singing the few blocks home
where a pickup white enough it's hard to see

is backing out of your drive to red-tag
more wrecked houses.

6.
The first blows the stripped-off screen
the spidered door window
                         strike you and pass on
through into wind. The red
UNSAFE FOR ENTRY tag though
                         and the neighbor's
soaked note—BOTH DOGS AT MY HOUSE
BOTH OK ARE YOU?—
                         land so squarely
on the brain they send you
dreaming on your feet. You close your eyes
flash of yellow countertop
                         the lapsed policy notice
white against it. You put a hand to the doorframe
and keep yourself from kneeling.
                         Drift of Fleet
howling low in her kennel. Rush of all the rain and flies
and roaring the ruined brickwork will be letting in.
Breathe   and fractures
                         liven in your ribs. Breathe out
moaning and your mind
                         won't hold you. What are you
anymore what's anyone   once a whole nerve works
of breaks is suffering
                         out in the walks and pavements
the fault lines waking   and no way left to ever
numb them back to sleep?

7.
                         The cracked cement down here
is giving off a migraine cool
                         the zag-shaped oak stick I'd
laid on the cup rim
                         is hurting where I've picked it up
stinging on into my wrist
                         and I know we're in now kinsman

this is the way
                    even if we have to go by gimp or sling to keep
the weight off a bone
                    even if we have to hum or sing
out loud to bear the ringing in our ears

Jim Roy   lost cause   true heart of mine we're in.

NOT MUCH MORE THAN A MOUTH

1.
Everything flickers   my keys and phone   the cup rim
and metal shelves
                the air smokes and unwinds
the water's already dreaming. I hold the cup close
enough to scry
              shaking the surface to a blur.
Nerves left over from the homes and so on loves
a name and face I had.
                Staring in I can half-
make out cloud banks   maybe drifts of fur or hair
but I have had enough of half.
              I'm sinking kinsman
all the way into you
                in your shadowy smear
at the cup's metal bottom
              I'm loosening
like an ink cloud   feeling you near   giving up
on the need to float
              letting your trouble through.

2.
A white shock in the dark window   a quick
fray in the nerves   and the cowboy wallpaper
lights up all around you and goes dim
                a few hours
since the skinny kid in horse pajamas glared your way
shuffling his way to the pullout couch
another hour until the nightmares
                but for now the rain
is shattering itself at the window with that flash
inside each drop
            hadn't you been taken up
lit through and through with weather
just to be thrown back down   sloughed off
a hated thing of the air
              a hailed-on casualty
passing these months as the neighbor's charge
watching cartoon lassos and hats
              light up
and go out in the miserable kid's room.

3.
I pull back my hand from the cup   let the surface smooth—
your features won't come clear in the water.
The smoke and buzzing hector me
                              and I admit
I have the photo out. I refuse to describe it.
Say it was a song—
               This used to be This used to be—
what good would it do to sing it?
                              I press my palm
back against the metal cup   reaching you again
by feel kinsman
                no matter if the water blurs and jumps.

4.
You drink sweet tea in the shade   the locust tree burning
with blooms   you can't stop the ice from jangling the glass
Darren's Skoal smile widens in his cap brim's shadow
his boat story's over   and you've learned to laugh
inhaling to protect your ribs   to keep your head
from throbbing   your chest seems blown open
at the breast bone   what swept you up and
dropped you here   wincing in shade against the sun?

Everyone who's put you up   cooked brisket for you
in a smoker   set cobbler cooling for you on a stove
is in this yard   you think of bites as fine and then as gone
as sweet smelling steam after you've breathed it   Thanks
you tell Helen   her white head trembling as she nods   and Carlos
who coughs and shrugs his bony shoulders when you say it
Thank you   your own voice alien   the sense of it mysterious.

If you can't be made of weather anymore   sweeping down as rain
over most of Comanche County   roaring gloriously   flashing
all through your heights
                    if you can't be a person on the earth
again either   a witcher and plumber of wells   if you can't
be Jim Roy with a house   or anything much at all to Ava
what kind of man is stripped to this   since no one held a gun
to your head when you walked out into the weather   if you
can't house yourself or your dogs   and merely being seen
sends weight and obligation into the neighborhood faces   if you
can't in all decency spare your hosts from the big-brimmed
killer running you through with a knife at night
opening the bedroom door on more than one morning

14

to find a mattress muffling the door against your yells
then what do you say you are   at the yard party Darren's
throwing in your honor   with your skull's zag-shaped ache
the patio's cracks and the splits in your ice   lights raying
out of everyone's head   and no one to describe this to
one of your dogs   the beagle   Mule   right at your side
but Fleet   with the one short leg   the greyhound who sprints
in wobbly circles and fetches anyway   leans into Darren
like his own   what could a person be who's not much more
than a mouth saying Thank you   Thanks a million until the yard's
empty   and it's dark in the kid's bedroom
                              and you're focused
on blacking out the image of the gun barrel at your head
Mule at your ankles   Fleet's warm breathing on your arm.

5.
With your face on wrong   your nightmared eyes
and fallen mouth   you let gray whiskers grow down
past your collarbone   you wear T-shirts wrong-side out
with the tags showing   most days purple or pink or green
get quick with a joke   and in a year at most you're not
Jim Roy anymore but Jimmy   swinging your arms loosely
singing to yourself   straw-hatted and in shades to cut
the throb of sun on day jobs drillers throw you sometimes
cleanup at well sites   unloading trucks   "Hey Jimmy"
they say   their grins careful   stiff   "how are them dogs?"
and you say   "a lot smarter and fatter than me"   and laugh
with them   inhaling   though your mouth doesn't show.

One afternoon   when you've changed out Darren's shop sink
and swept up after   you slip off with the dogs into pastures
north of town   to witch for water in low acreage   out of sight
the cut branch tugs   and various wells you sited and piped
come back to you   the gardens still green after all these years
the clear tap water   kids and dogs out in the sprinklers
maybe you haven't come to nothing after all   the ones
named for you chiming in mind like song titles as you witch—
the Royal James   the Giant Jim   the JR   the Gushing Jimbo.

You mark the strongest pulls with rocks   and when the branch
seems spent you toss it   Fleet half-sprints   half-hops
in her odd way to fetch it   you accept it from her   give it
to Mule for chewing   walk back down to the willow draw
and cut a new one.
                         An hour's witching and it never pulls

as dead to water as a fencepost. You know to just lay it down
something off about it   something wrong   but you wing it
far ahead with your good arm   Fleet almost gets to it   catches
her good front leg in the snake hole   and goes down yelping.

6.
The vet bills arrive and arrive. Darren writes the checks
saves the dog and the leg   never mind the braced joint.
Odd jobs could never touch the number. You're finished
more a burden than a person
                                  and the note you leave
bedside says   Darren I thank you for my life and Fleet's
I'm leaving the dogs for you   you're the one that
deserves them. I hope your boy can do better now
with his mom still gone   and all he give up on my account.

7.
And you move on then into legend   where at first it seems
you've driven off to shoot yourself with your uncle's gun
you always have it in the truck   but every few weeks
for more than a year   envelopes with two or three twenties
keep arriving   addressed to Darren and Dogs   and it's clear
from postmarks you must be drifting west   lake town
to mountain town to plains.
                            When the envelopes stop coming
you're swept up   decades removed from here   into whatever
calling it is   that strips you to shame and skin   and in time
to less than that
                      barely more than a bad taste in the mouth
of someone old who'd spit and name you as a moocher   a loser
who left his dogs.
                 Until restlessness or kinship or who knows what
draws you back to Lawton   to be conjured in a cup of water.

8.
I never could divine a well   but with the zag
of an oak stick in one hand
                        the other around the cup
I have something like your touch. I shake away
the whining at my ears
                raise the wavering face
in the water to my mouth
                     and drink it down completely.

Your fractures shine all through me.
                                        I pocket my effects
blow out the wicks
                    grope my way to the railings
and even if it does feel Jim boy
                              an awful lot like a calling—
the oak stick's light enough it's pulling upward—
I start climbing the ladder stairs in the dark.

SORRY AS WE ARE

    1.
Brother out of our mind   into the full-on
world we climb   that shocking heat upon us
one hand up against the sun
                        an iron earthquake
slamming shut behind us on our doings.
Nothing left in the grass but glare
shaped like a door.
                  Had a cellar ever even been there?
Out of the hold and into the pull we
squint and make our way   the oak stick in hand
and a bellyful of roving   a pocket buzzing
as messages rush back in the phone.
                         Locusts
are loud at it in the burr oaks   and the slab has been
dozered clean of a house   save the cracks
and pipe holes—
              walking it you feel
in your heel bones the hard featureless heat
where the rooms and dreams had been.
                          The sheen
is blinding if you face it   and if you close your eyes
not even a whiff of dog   or the ghosted wind it
once made wagging.
                What good anyway
is a calling?
          Just stepping down to the root-heaved street
starts up the knee that had gone easy all morning
on the throbbing.
              But for well or ill kinsman I've imped
my limp on yours   and now we sweat and feel our way
and shine like slugs in the full-out sun.

    2.
What say we slip off into the shade of this bait shop?

The door's long gone but the Coke machine's still on.

Finally get that heat off our head the miles off our feet.

It's dark in here but put your hand down in that concrete tank.

Even in the dry you can feel the shadows of minnows and shad that used to shiver in the aerated water.

And don't a Coke taste as fine right now as tin cup water back at Trevor's well?

It's dark enough in here you could about be there in his no-window pump shack now.

Or be six on a dead-dark road about to light the sparkler in a Nehi bottle.

Or twenty with your eyes closed. Feeling her hair ease in all around your breathing.

Except for that sick that's in your face that shock or crazy or whatnot.

What say we break out the phone about now?

Light up some guitar in here some conspiracy politics. A little sexy stuff a little Wrigley Field.

You can forget about that sick sometimes if you just keep scrolling.

You can look up roads you used to drive or friends you used to have.

You can post a photo of a big bright doorhole in a wall of dark.

You can touch here for help if you need to. You can phone home if you have one.

3.
Shuffling through the bar ditch weeds
soaked and rank already   my head blazing
needing a ride and afraid to flag one down—

I can see over the fields a haze that's
come a thousand miles to show us
half the forest world's on fire.

The shed and silo waver in a blur I once
believed was only heat. Clouds to the south
swirl in on clouds   circulating

hail and lightning   working up their fury.
The swallowed face in my belly is also out
troubling the minds of two whirlwinds

harrowing the furrows   churning inward
suffering their smoke of sand   inhaling
shredded ropes and sacks   but what could ever

satisfy the hole at the eye of what you are?
The huge one blows on through the fence
a low roaring stays behind   a tractor's

stopped where the air clears. The glassed-in
driver has the fierce gasping look
of a drowner   and I almost call out *Brother*!

But he cuts the engine   opening
the high door   and I can hear hate radio
up loud in there as he steps down

all that sound behind him   driving him
my way like a wind. I can't make out words
though I understand completely   *Stranger*

I will shoot you if I need to. He yells out
Can I help you?   and I don't speak or move
but I have my thumb out toward the road.

Then a flash is rushing over the weeds
a truck is idling   and I understand—
the rumbling's come for me. I turn

and see the dark-haired driver   two huge
mongrels in the seat beside him. He shouts *Abajo*
pointing to the empty flatbed. *Back there.*

The one approaching yells Can I help you?
The driver shouts *A dónde vas*—I close my eyes
feeling the way the oak stick pulls   blurt out *North*!

jump up on the truck bed   and crouch   my back
to the generator strapped there   the watcher
standing at the fence a long time as we roll.

4.
Wheat rows shudder by   side roads blur and rattle. Anyone
with teeth and bones would understand the ground
has had enough of us   all the way down
to the shale.
              Sorghum now. A shack with a cow
half in it. Boot prints leading out   survivors
staying one day's work ahead of famished.
                                   All this brutal
wind that's worse than useless. How hot can sun get?

Maybe just hum a little and shield your eyes.
Maybe hold that feed sack on your head unless
you like it blistered.
                    Just rattle like that a while.
In the sack shade. The oat smell. Until it's nigh well
third grade again.
                  Nigh well high up on the rumbling
trailer next to you Ofelia   and your brothers.
Sliding off at your shack's dirt yard. Straightway
to the roped tire to swing you
                          a gold girl over the cotton rows.
Your five brothers grinning   skinny and angry
a shade of gold called brown. We all knew it was wrong
for a kid to be there white   but not why.
                                  Caramel eyes
quick at math   you only stayed in school one season.
If you're alive   I glimpsed you then   I see you now
jarred and blistered with my eyes closed on this rig—

smaller than I was and brighter   offering what you had
hot wind   leaves rushing by   your quick smile
and flying hair—

5.
What say we collect ourself here on the underpass's shady side a while?

Lean the oak stick on the concrete and mop our eyes and try to come to terms.

Lost now on the way to where?

Sky with all that high white smoke. Mosquitoes all over us. The ground rumbling.

Far off a couple of dogs. Not half a chance of rubbing their backs or handling their ears.

Maybe just duck our head a minute and give it up. Sorry as we are.

Who didn't have the sense to stay in out of a tornado. Who couldn't maintain enough wherewithal to feed our own animals.

And climbed up into all this again. The ladder wiped out behind in a crash of glare.

Lost here brother an overpass for a roof and thunderheads swelling in the southerly haze.

Dry lightning then the dim roar. In a while we'll flag another ride and maybe have a bed.

But growing up crop to crop in shacks. In and out of school. Did she even live?

One time in downtown Tulsa a squall came on and all at once a dozen bony grimed ones were under the awnings.

One with his gray hand out near some covered stairs. Passersby climbing on toward the brand names.

Kids already up top throwing nickels in the fountain.

Maybe widening the mind to misery can tune it to what's right.

I'm heavy into yours kinsman but there's more. Pulling us farther in.

Don't believe it's traffic. Knowing all these houses are riding on a shuddering in the ground.

So shaky or not we get up from the shade. The low sun brutal in the haze.

And let our mind give in so the pull and zag have ahold of us. And the tremors.

And from here on find our way by glare and smoke.

BURNING MAN

1.
I swipe my blistered head   one eye on
thunderheads coming for the sun.

Not a breath without the smoke smell. Not one
rumbling without the trouble in it.

Feelingly I reach my oak stick out. And by
wince or pull
                by a nerveworks of fractures
I get what passes. A ghosted semi
rattles by   the pickup in a film of grime.
A half-mile off one high crow floats
                                a sedan
changing lanes below   all the chromes flashing—
an ache like foil on a filled tooth.

In no time it arrives for me   a silver
Chrysler. I feel the heat of it idling
a door gleams open
                and I know—
smoke rolling out in the slant sun.

2.
Heat-blind I lean in. A woman's voice. You can ride with me   if you
  don't mind some smoke.

The seat's plush. It's cool and dim. I can just make out the cigarette
  her manicured hand. Considering how I have to smell the smoke's a
  godsend.

She says Your head looked like it was on fire   and I begin to see her
  dark-complected   her hair straightened   red-streaked.

I say I'm widening my mind. She looks me up and down   studies the
  oak stick at my side   her face gone weary   breathes out a
  scalding sound.

A man of your years she says   reaching back to the cooler for a water
  should not be burning up out in the sun.

With all that smoke I knew for sure I say   and drink   grateful
    ready for her messages.

She shakes her head   mouths something. Sets her forward stare. Puts
    in ear buds and accelerates   smoke blowing out as we go.

3.
When the head-throb's gone I can
hear a rumbling under the AC that's
all there is suspending us at seventy.

Just some silence would drop us
to the rushing pavement   the driver's
contempt seems absolute   and by

no means am I true enough
to be braving the wakened world
again   peering out of my sockets

like a fugitive through a slot. Not so
long ago I was a boy who'd love
a thistle weed if it had a miller on it.

The storm's green light and far-off
flashes have reached the oaks
and pump jacks   you can feel

the pressure dropping   and it isn't
so much that you understand
what's coming   as that you've already

known it to strip man and tree
to their skin   and leave them standing....

4.
In the dark now brother I have
you close   and what a frightful
witness squad we are   with no

legs down in the door well   no torso
to speak of   and all this storm-
bashed ruin   this abandonment

of dogs to haunt us. You'd think
dialing in some radio might help—
the driver in her ear buds

never flinches—but it's Christian
Christian   country   Christian
country   Christian   classic rock.

So with used-up music going   rolling on
under a front that towers   flashing
and doesn't rain   kinsman we're worn

so bare the dark shows through.
And a voice that half-passes for
what we are   whispers *Used to be.*

The mind's-eye white of a sky-lit room
the backs of her olive-soft legs   the high
almost yodeled tones of hounds that

aren't here   howling   guilts and grievances
harms floating with no body   just semblances
and words   as speed propels us

eastward   suspended by the grace
of a few feet over the blacktop   ceaselessly
whispered to. *A lost home   a cellar—*

injury what are you   that you tell yourself
relentlessly   as if against some
doubt you're real? Kinsman   brother

only you seem genuine   close enough
I barely know your pulse from mine. Ruin
what's left of you but what you gave me—

wince   shudder   dream? The disposition
of a shallow-nerved tooth   fine-tuned
to the weather. Maybe it never

comes to nothing after all. A flash
our heads and shoulders   those suspended
in the other lane   all up and down the road

shine manifestly   and are lost again
even before the noise arrives   levitators
all of us   thinking of our quick   bright

confines   ignoring the massive
shadow we're dissolved in. No more.
In the blackout I can sense how

all this breathing feeds weather that keeps
funneling and coming for us   how all
the driving is unsettling hills that weren't

quite finished anyway with being an ocean.
The lightless droning floats us   and yet this late
there's so much sinking. How heavy

can a body can get as the pull takes hold—
brother are you with me? The undertow's
in earnest   and we're going where it goes.

5.
Hey Radio she says. Hey Burning Man   and I'm awake. We're parked
    a windshield full of hotel lights.

She says You'll need a bed   watching me without blinking. My salty
    clothes   my red hands in my lap. My kinsman nowhere visible.

Not at my house she says. I have people to think about. Her bracelets
    shine   and her jogging suit.

I open my door   all that light   and stand. Saying I think I know you
    not to her outfit or skin   but to where she's in behind her eyes.

She considers this   my clothes and oak stick   eventually my eyes. She
    takes her card from the dash and offers it   still considering.

I slide it in a pocket   sense its messages coming through by touch
    thank her for the ride

and limp on into the lobby   where Amanda with the nametag   with
    chalk skin and drifting lipstick   types me in for the night   eying
    my branch familiarly

mentioning her felon brother the water witcher   her husband studying
   the prophesies   doing time in Talladega   her nightly Ativan
   that's like swallowing a miracle.

Upstairs   dry flashes at the window   her angled smile still with me if I
   blink   I rinse my shirt out   hang it on a lamp

and listening to the far-off shuddering   I flip the lights off   let my
   mind go into all the darkness over Tulsa   and blank out on the
   clean bed on my back.

Made in the USA
Middletown, DE
09 April 2019